Singing the Seasons

Singing the Seasons

by

Helen Fujimoto

Cyberwit.net

India

For Akimi

with love and gratitude for his life and work
and for our life together

The Tree

Holding earth's history
roiled, twisted,
blasted by lightning
split by earthquake
and at the last sullied
by human building
a thousand years
the tree stands
too huge, too roiled
to be so
simply called
a tree

shaken through
ancient storms,
ravaged in grain
twisted, grimaced
Tree holds the earth
in place
struck open
to the heart
the dark interior cave
yet holds huge bulk,
ancient wood mountain
links earth to sky

Contents

Note to Readers

"For what is a poem but a hazardous attempt at self-understanding: it is the deepest part of autobiography."
— Robert Penn Warren, as quoted in the
New York Times, 12th May 1985

This book grew out of a core group of poems that I wrote during the days of my husband's illness and death and in the months and years of grieving after that. I found, during the worst times of hospitalization for his cancer treatment, and even more with the approach of his death, that the way I could tap into the love and grief that lay under the busyness and stress of visits to the hospital, and the grim march of losses and diminishments, was to write poetry. And after his death, in that bleak tunnel of grief, it was poetry that kept me alive to myself. Those poems seemed to need some context, but not the whole story of our lives. Around that core of poems written in the living through Akimi's illness and death, I gathered together the poems I had written in and about different periods of our lives, and in the compiling, I came to see and better understand the cycle of my own life, hence this book's title.

I met Akimi on the campus of the Universiti Malaya in Kuala Lumpur, where we each went to study for our Masters degrees—he from Japan, I from Australia. We became friends and then partners, and after three years in Malaysia, went together to Adelaide, where Akimi undertook his PhD. That entailed another year of research in Malaysia, before returning to Australia to complete the work and welcome our eldest son. In 1980, we came to Japan so that Akimi could apply for a job in his former university, and after six months living with his parents in a Niigata village, we settled in Nerima Ward in Tokyo.

Our daily life through following decades was lived, reflected, and sometimes scrambled through the double lens of English and Japanese. This meant coming to terms with differences not just of opinion and ways of living, but also fundamental ways of being and speaking or not speaking—the hidden silences and codes that hide behind and between the words of any language. I was also influenced at a fundamental level by the knowledge that I am not native to this society. Brought up on a farm in Australia, I have been fortunate to live in central Tokyo in a convenient apartment building situated right next door to a working farm. The trees of the farm are my backdrop to life in the city, and their acre of farmland allows me a wider view of the sky. It was through a deepening relationship with the natural world and a growing sense of belonging to the land itself that opened a different way for me to explore the experience of belonging in Japan.

Because of the subject matter of some of the poems, I refer here to specific Japanese funeral customs, which take up a much deeper part of ongoing daily life, and which were part of my own daily life. Soon after a death, a wake is held in the evening, and the funeral service is held the following morning. The body is cremated at the crematorium, often located within the funeral home. In a ceremonial act after the cremation, close family members gather to pick up the bones with special long metal chopsticks and place them in an urn. The urn is placed in a box of *hinoki* cypress wood and covered in white brocade. The box and the large photo of the deceased used at the wake and funeral are taken from the altar to the family home and placed on the family altar. Family and friends continue to visit in the first days and weeks after the death, to burn incense and offer prayers at the family altar. There is usually a ceremony on the forty-ninth day after death to inter the bones in the family grave. Some people choose not to follow this time line—I myself did not—and keep the bones on the altar at home until they feel ready to undertake the internment ceremony.

The poems are grouped in roughly chronological order, with Part I, "The Way We Were" being about Akimi's and my meeting and the early years of our marriage. Most of the poems in Part II, "Weathering", were written in the middle years of my life when I was struggling to balance family and career. The poems of the next two parts, "Parting" and "Grieving", were written during the ten months of Akimi's illness and death and the months and years following. The last part, "Reweaving Life", is about my acceptance of grief, learning to live alone, and slowly growing to integrate grief with the joys and sorrows of continuing life.

The Way We Were

playing ball
with the world
dance in spring rain

springing
wet grass
early morning swing

long cool drink
the blessing
of your being

Maps

Listening
I hear the lie
of your land
get a feel
for how you move
in your world
what sign posts
what landmarks
light or darken
your mindscape

easily I see
your map
blind to
my own

in momentary
flashes
I remember
the view is a map
for reference only
not to be taken
for the actual lie
of our land

Different Languages

What is this
missing meaning
telling and listening
to jokes where
who knows
where and when
to laugh

living side by side
in worlds of such different
colour and configuration
it's hard even to picture
the other

suddenly
then
an explosion
a word, a smile,
a glance exchanged,
this I — you — we
understand

Parallel Lines

Speaking
now that language
now this

my mind forgets
the ways between

loses a word
to bring the one
to the other

baulks at the barrier
of moving

from here to there —
you to me —

by two such
different vehicles

Your Country

How to make my place
not to say mark
in a place I don't belong
I wasn't born here
don't speak the language
grew on different food
an alien
yet here
I've chosen to live

how to make my place
what do I need
to change
what create

import my own desires
fresh-ground morning coffee
hedges of rosemary
rye toast conceding to
local custom with miso
or nori

planting alien seeds
on local ground
watching them grow
growing with them
slowly into
accustomed use.

I place my gods and
goddesses and
with the placing
create new space
to hold
my own spirit
and sense
of being

Journey

Song line
starts with
a small sound
a smile a sigh
a smell a memory
spark
catches and trills
along the wire

a new story
beginning in
deep slow
humming
running
the lines
of the body

melodies sing
stories start
trip wires along
memory-roads
opening new
views paths
flash points
for new ways
of being

Coming and Going

You left this
morning too early
jolted from
short sleep
to move
body-wake and
sip the sweetness
of lips goodbye
hugging through
the passing door

now I sit all astray
out of my rhythm.
Left undone
I strive to pull my
threads to the loom
get to my weaving

my pattern wavers
astray on this first
Saturday of autumn,
watching children
lovers families
hand-in-hand and
old lone people
walk
faster than
their past

Return

Whirlwind hugs
in through the door,
"I'm back."

bags dumped
washing out
swags of dirty clothes

boxes of rich smelling pickles
fresh-picked cucumbers
tomatoes eggplants potatoes

goodly portion
of the summer harvest
spilling across the narrow
kitchen floor of this Tokyo
apartment — offshoot of a
Niigata village farm-house

The Dance

Your performance is
always high energy
dancing on the ropes,
whipping up the air
into a frenzy
of action
then withdrawal
into concentration
so deep you don't
know your own
body but that
your fingers do your bidding
on the keyboard
your princess
I call it now
I used long
since to be
your keyboard

for now you are
frame and pillar
shelter-steady
holding open space
for my daily acts of
keeping caring cleaning,
teaching loving being
yourself absent
absorbed in
worlding

Sharing Life

I sing my song
you sing your song
separate solos
time after time
entwining

sometimes too long
between times
the sense
of shared life
richness of being
in met glance
lip curve
passing pat

you preserve your deepest
feeling a long way down
so far maybe
you don't yourself
know where it is

future-focused
the five-year plan
the dream
the next action
all that work is
the center of your life

planning others' lives
making systems
changing things
rattling the bars

no time to remember
how we got here or
spin tales of love and
maybe dangerous to look
too close at
the source
of the dream

different paces
of loving advancing
retreating dancing
in step then missing it
all together —
this business of
being married
while loving
in and around
and between

Finding Each Other

You sink so deep
into whatever you are doing
words child cries things dropped
nothing reaches you
then job done
energy released
you leap to your feet
ready in a minute and call
"what's keeping you! I'm done!"

my rage played out over
the years to a present calm
after all knowing you
hold the sense of me
without show
deep in your life
when called it rises to the
surface and meets me at
the place I need

You learned to break
out of "shoulds and
musts" knowing them as
bondage that might kill
you, given free rein

come now to know
it is after all possible
to choose and do what is
deeply enjoyable
as part of the dream
the passion of
a mind-guided life,
responding still
to passion as it comes
to meet you

I learn through deep hard
lessons to find and value
my own wisdom
as for me second to none
holding to my path and
now at last
grown into your country
your language
I come back to find
myself   strong
at the root of it
with you

River Rapids

I think as myself but
feel in relation to you
holding deep the knowing
of our thirty years lived
branching from the root.
We tangled and tore
but still together knew
the other as root and home
now past the rapids
I feel deep respect and know
wordless understanding
of our joint creation

when the rocks were sharpest
the current most dangerous
I covered myself
with unknowing
hiding
from myself
the fear
of losing
safety
our boat
myself
you

remembering
now I wonder
at the depth
and strength
of this
unknowing

Way Station

I don't remember
how
I got here
didn't look back

the climb was hard
I watched my feet
and the rocks ahead

now at a plateau
I look down at the
way I've come
and wonder
at distant clouds
and the long-ago
plains
far below

Togetherness

A call a question,
meets an answering
in me — considered
or not it wells up
from long years of
being together and
understanding the
ground lie direction
of feeling

passion changes
moves but still
resides in body
and mind
though long usage
and the body's
age reworks the
expression of it

Weathering

floating rain
damp train station
slow walk home in the dark

red wine on
a working day
rainy afternoon

concentration of winter
walkers wrapped
in hopes of spring

unexpected affection
under the eaves
crows canoodling

spider webs
after rain
pockets full of jewels

Late Autumn

Leaves turn
and fall
coming all adrift
senses slip
out of focus
in the shuddering
cold of coming
winter

I look for rest
but roam astray
between then
and now
meeting parts of me
on the way,
not knowing
the road to take

there's a left-over
maze of tracks
hidden under
dry leavings
nothing to show
how I come
to be
here
now

North Wind

North wind
roars in
tree tops
I huddle my head
against the coming
winter
scuffing through
rustled piles of
browning leaves

last year's
spring passion
now a lost fling
spinning down
the wind in fall
to settle
moulder
blend and
become earth

Weather

I sit with grey clouds
feeling it
the morning
under a cloud

the sun would make it
easier to shine
I feel the declining
to move

as an ache
an old pain
in part of
my heart that still

keeps the sunshine
of other times
of womanhood

A Long Cold Winter

Opening to the light
warm of early
spring sunshine

it's been a long
cold winter
not over yet
frigid fingers
still struggle
with obdurate keys

stuck in congealed
feelings cold
with old fears
blank about
the future

wind chill
shuts down
the heart
grey wipes
the mind

my legs stiffen
into aging
slowing
in the blast

stumbling over
the stubs of
things undone
and drifts
of dried up
dreams

Interlude Before Spring

Suddenly warmed
in smoky clouds
of humid air
winter memories
fade

bodies long
tightened
against the chill
relax and
ease open
to the growing
warm through
ice chill to
blossom
burst

deadened branches
quicken
into spring
and bud
by bud
tree after
tree
breathes
full and fuller
into blossom

Change

The body world
is moving
towards
spring and summer
but parts of it
can't keep up
the pace

in rifts and cracks
and shaded corners
lie old heaps of snow
iced rock-hard
smeared with dirt
holding out
against the general
warming

Forest Breathing

The forest breathes
gently
after rain
small birds sing
crickets call
leaves slide off
drops to
wet-leaf carpets
below

sudden wind
lifts   turns
leaves to toss
and scatter
rain drops
down
on my hair

strung wide
swinging gently
webs
glisten with jewels
each threaded
rung spread in
intricate geometry
of silver linking
the reach between

tree trunks glisten,
the shining streams
watering
dappled bark
alight
with new
patterning

Spring Meditation

Sitting
on a park bench
in early spring
feet set on
still cool
earth
littered
with winter's
decaying needles

above me
sun-lit
foliage
wind-swayed
gold and green
in front
ruffled water
sun-shined
into dance

my green passing
to red brown gold
ready
to fall
exalting
all colour
birthing
and dying
with new green

An Old Song

Thrumming, reeling
humming with the
ending song — body
soul snatches time
behind the moments
of lived life
to rest the spirit
in deep knowing

this song was long
reaching far down
beyond sound
and sense

the echoes of memory
strands in the body
slowly deepen
to the low
steady humming
that sings
the rhythm
of the soul

Life Forms

Glimpsing my reflection
in shop windows
graying hair lined face
glasses just askew
unremarked
unremarkable

I feel the inner life
of joy rising
the love of this
breath
air movement
flower
face
sunlight playing
shadows on pavement,
in every cell
a breathing joy
and radiance

this unremarked
ordinary shape
carrying such
wonderment
fizzing with joy

I look in wonder
at others as
ordinary
and ask
do they too
carry this
same sense
of deep
cell-dancing
awe of
mystery

Word Smithing

Strange for one
who distrusts words
and struggles so
to speak
what lies deep
distrusting the unmooring
as a rending of perception
separating sound and act
from feeling

that now I turn
after all
this long
crenellated time
to words
not spilling out
but hauling
seizing smithing

to out is a relief
an emptying
still deepening
freeing my sense
of time passed
worn living
breathing meaning
with dream making

distrust the ready flow
too smooth
not well
connecting the twined
strands of meaning that
make up the vines of
these my years and days

the weight and shape
of a word
the feel of its veins
the place I reach
to grasp it
is both measure
and part
of the act of
making meaning

Why Remember

Another day slipping
forward from the mist
today I see only of myself
the many things I have
put on hold
years moments minutes
of think and write and do

then all the ways I find
this too is not true
not on hold but accepted
lived and for some while
buried deep
held until
the time is right

changing tides and
seasonal flow
uncover these
ambiguous treasures
beacons and signs of knowing
once shelved for ripening
now washed in light

with the setting down
of one foot and then
the other
each reaching
into my unknown
this stepping
becomes
the path

Partings

one breath
long pause
is it time to go

please yourself
you always said
even dying

these words of mine
a net
to catch the tears

my friend, when you
read these, I'll be long gone
winter snows

Earthquake

Molten plates
deep below the surface
shake and move and
burn slow
deep strong
quiet and long

then suddenly erupt
burst roiling up
flame and molten rock
to a surface
shocked and shaken
from daily calm
now to face
a new configuration
of the mind's reality

Remembering a Friend's Tears

Evening convocation of crows
cawing and wheeling
on the wind of early autumn —
the trees sway and rustle
above me golden brown
evening sun glints

I sit on the bench
under browning larches
remembering her words,
her tears her hugs
despair tingling outrage
"life was not meant to be
like this — we were supposed
to be happy — the struggle
wears me down"

her spilling tears
spring my defiance
"I'm alive — we are alive
we can fight even now
for what we thought
we wanted"

let the tears fall
like brown leaves
come to their time
this year's harvest
will never come
again — hold out
your hands to grasp
the wind — see —
it moves everything
in its path — like Spirit
it moves and you cannot
see it but from
that which it moves

let this wind
blow through
my heart
whip whirl
scattered
leaves
into patterns
falling into
a path
carpet for
the coming
days

Pain

The times are set
all to do — attend —
be there — accept it —
wait for it — pay for it
come back
lie on the bed
teeth gritted, back
bent forward over
the cushion pressed
against the pain

I see the set lips
jutted jaw
tiredness
of bent shoulder
feel the pain of it
flinch clench and look
away — see the sharpness
of bones and pale skin —
my heart clenches and
opens again and then again
I put the glass of water
into your outstretched hand

The Door

You walk into
the room
close the door
I can see you through
the glass — you don't
see me looking

you close your
face your eyes
your hands
and sit
quiet
holding pain

there is no way
into this room
I shut the front door
walk
rapidly
away

today I will
buy flowers
to celebrate
defeat

Getting Out

Getting out
for a walk
locking the door
on a pile of need
to go shake make
change move
do create

going out for a walk
locking the door
walking fast down
the side road
to the temple
to pray
ringing the bell
fierce and clear

easing then
into the sounds of late
autumn evening —
golden light
slanting low through trees
now yellow and brown
birds chirping and wheeling
in the light space before sundown

I sit on a cut-off tree trunk
to ease my heart
feeling the squeezed
tightness gentle
and open
to greet
what may come
with this
golden evening

My Heart Aches

My heart
aches
for the heart
behind
your locked door

so much love
held in
locked down
searing —

waiting words
not said
not given
"too late"
you said,

your breaking
heart
locked
behind the
unyielding door

Locked

Under the visions
the plans the excitement
of meetings and trips
lie unexpressed
secret tunnels
of pain regret
fear
why didn't I
why didn't you
couldn't we now
is it really
too late

words rise up
in the heart
and die unspoken
on lips locked
into patterns
of silence

what light can
dying bring
to living
how unlock
the reservoirs
of hidden love
for these
the young ones
looking to the
future but still
dragging chains
of hidden pain

Space

Clouds slide by the glass
I revel in blue sky and steel
feel myself sloughing off
unwashed dishes peeling
balconies and potatoes
reveling in a short freedom
of cubed and bounded space
I have nothing to do here
that is the call of it
alone behind the glass

no need to watch
pain rise and clench
no need to imagine
wonder how to draw
out the tired spirit
soothe the ache of
a soon to die body
no need to transmute
wait serve hold catch
the falling of body
or spirit

here I can ease out
my own soul,
let the tears
rise and
freely
fall

Trapped

by success
in a place where
every other
demands
a favor a job
a chance to help
change the world
or someone's life

stop, go home,
end it — rest —
but the net closes
in as more
and more
knock on the door

unspoken words
close in
weave around
the tired heart
a deep cocoon
of silence

Riding the Subway

I got a seat on the
fast train doing the
crossword looking at
sleeping fellow travelers

feeling the quick
stabs to my heart
they come often now
I turn quietly
to my heart
feel the beat
of it slow
calming easing

now I take
into my hand
fears pushed aside
look see feel
what my heart
whispers

hold it, taste it
as it rises
in your throat
this is the time
here is the place
anywhere now
to call death
to your side
ease gently into the
loving and the
loss that is
to come

and in the grieving
wash the heart with
tears that ease
strengthen and heal
who knows what of
that I have hidden even
perhaps especially
from myself

and getting off
the train
coming up
into sky and ground
I taste the sweetness
of the air and
feel earth
steady under my feet

Looking at the Road

Seeing feeling
how things should
could be
what needs doing
but caught
snagged in clinging
pride passion
all pushing to the end
that we rush to

the aching heart
sees the cost
feels the pain of
the self's neglect
powerless to fight
shadow
or even maybe
to see until
the very end

the heart breaks
under the weight of
love
suddenly recognized
self-hidden

tears
unbidden
melt the icy threads
break boundaries
to freedom
forgiveness
the lost joy
the release
and birth
of death

Breath of God

I whispered
in your ear
as you lay dying
Breath of God
Breath of God

Now I lie alone
on your bed
looking out at
the cedar forest
Breath of God
Breath of God

Wind moves
the crowns of
giant trees
I remember and feel
Breath of God
Breath of God

Grieving

opening the front door
I catch it
the whiff of your incense

bright candle flame
your room
empty now

hands in my pockets
feeling the grip
of your hand

Each Morning

67

I rise and walk
to your room,
light the candle
and three sticks
of sandalwood
incense

sometimes I ask
these three for me
or one for each
of us who are
separately left
you went away
first from them
then from me

I stay alone
with the work
of your leaving
each mourning
morning with
each new candle
and the growing
pile of ash
new ground
of being

Possession

Your chopsticks in the mug
on the kitchen sink
standing with mine
I cannot move
nor your towel
washed clean
hanging unused
on the bathroom rail

dark corners of cupboards
all contents turned out
upended drawers spill
decades-old letters
mine to you
yours to me
piles slowly drawn together
a weaving of memory
seeing how this weaving
could be a project
not knowing yet if
it will be mine

clothes
mine and yours
piece by piece
ceremonial workplace
home space
each cloth calling up
time space place
of our lived life

my hands move
of themselves
neatly fold and pile
to give or throw —
I wonder at
the difference
between two pieces
of old cloth

that
I throw away
in a breath
this
catches
my breath
in a rain
of tears

Shifting World

The life we shared
friends lovers partners
forty years gone with your going
I am alone in this place
tearing it apart with my hands
to hold to what feels true
mourn and throw out
lost meanings
give away what feels
rightful to give

not in words but in
the picking up of things
files books dishes cups
the stuff of our shared life
slow painful wild, weeping
I move among these things
each moment aware
an earthquake could smash
this and all things
to chaos

in your room the paper cranes
still hang
half burned with you
half remain above your photo and
the heavy box that holds your bones
the paraphernalia of death
candle holder bowl of ash
wooden tongue to strike
the ringing bowl
in prayers for the soul

your bones are here
the things around
are changing
my relationship with each
myself
the memories
of you
our shared life
deepening and flowing
into the dark

Your Shadow

I join the party
your shadow
at my back

what they want
is the shadow
to remember
draw strength
use for an ending
in new beginning

mourn your absence
offer gratitude
too late
in a place where they
may find a trace
of you

so I join the party
your shadow
at my back
to be as may be
for affirmation

After

Sharing this space
opening all the doors
lighting the candle
I receive the gift
of messages
words of love
unexpected treasures
slipped
into my heart

they come
to mourn
pray and pay
respect
offer gratitude
for favors received
life courses opened
decades of working
towards a shared vision

how do I hold
this tribute
harvest
after
your passing
the offerings
all fruits
of your
doing

Container

An empty glove
hangs on the wire
puffed still
with the shape
of once warmed
fingers
curled still
turning to shake
the other hand
still circled
to protect the fingers
as they reached
for life

Naked in Winter

Looking for
a way through
I come to these trees
stripped thin and bare
sky-reaching
scraggy in early
spring sunshine

meta sequoias
at the end of
a long winter
their nakedness
catches my heart
and calls out
a kindred sense

bared to the
elements
battered by
winter and early
spring storms
pain the only
sign of growth

the greening
not yet
visible

Human

All the holding
of humans
husband children
job place
lost
gone

in this now here
between empty
moments
swinging wide
open in space
breathing into my roots

I find my soul
surrounded
beamed upon
cradled by friends
brothers and sisters

by blood or not
soul journeying company
leaning into the
rich tapestry of
connection

Where

I miss you
here now
in this place
alone
and alone is ok

the way I miss you
is an ache
a not-there-ness
that used to
be filled even
by your absence

this final absence
is today
void
of any sight or
membrance
of you

I search
sometimes
inside of me
what I find is
not your
long-fingered
hands
not your wide
shoulders
narrow hips

but a sense
of endurance
the long view
the passion
and the care
that fueled

you
I find
sometimes
in me

Double Grief

You have gone
away
out
at least
of my sight

the jagged edges
of new grief
are ground
in minutes
and sharp days

torn from the port
of the old life
now out to sea
I lose sight
and memory of
familiar shores

the sharp and
precarious memory
of you fades
misting a once
solid seeming life

double grief
the vivid loss of you
and of
the jagged edge
of felt memory

Remembering

Grey sky
steady rain
the ending
of summer

in the air
everywhere
crickets spring
in wet grass

I hold this day
in my hand
dark now
and quiet

remembering
that day
your passing
rain falls

Alone Now

I live
alone in rooms
large now
as they were small
when we were
four here
I hold the space
purge the contents
shining debris
of our life

living alone
fuels who I am
growing into
here   now   and
tomorrow
for all my
days and the
days of my
children
and their
children's
lives

the presence in my
soul of the voices
of those I love
and those who

love me
now are the fuel
for my growing
gently   harshly
in fits and jerks
and glides
to the ending
of this life's
day

now in this
quiet space
of my home
my soul finds
fuel to grow
into who
I am always
being

Reweaving Life

alone on the path
I feel you
beside me

perfect package
unfolding
new buds

pile of broken shards
my life   sunlight
shines into diamonds

Colour of Tears

I wonder
seeing myself
put earrings into
earlier pierced holes
still holding open
just enough
and wearing colours
blue, mauve, pink
purple and green
not to mean
I'm done
grieving

the tears rise
even as I smile
stand again
at the very edge
of the precipice
feel the joy of
being alive
in the world
you left
before all was done
still struggling to
protect your creations
and me

Moment of Freedom

I claim this
minute
this real
this deep
pulsing life
this joy
of breathing aromas
exchange of smiling
life in the eyes
of passing strangers
this fragility
this feeling
sense
being
living
loving
dancing
sun shining
on green leaves
tossed in
high winds
moving spirit
love
the sense even as
and because
it will be
lost

Wellspring

I throw it all away
in the loving
the leaving
and in the arriving
moment by moment
letting go of myself
stepping off into
the next unknown
the special kind of
peace beyond
events of feeling
good or bad

this business
of being
with myself
at peace
with this moment
essential to
this moment
the wellspring

Light and Shadow

Daily round
the wrapping of a blanket
to hide from the dark
morning coffee
pulling garden weeds
cooking the evening meal
even this
the creation of a poem

to pretend
the wolf is not
gnawing at my heart
pretend these are not
ways to hold back
the dark

until I see
that dark
in me
counterpart
partner of my light

All the Ways

I love this
being alive
I see — reel
at such beauty
rage and stir
all the ways
I hate resent grieve
weep shout pray
prostrate

all the ways
this world
is shuddering
all the ways
people hurt and
are hurt to despair

all the ways
the scars hide
our pain
all the ways
eyes send messages
of hope grief love
all the ways
love turns to fear

all the ways
to open the doors
reach the hearts
all the ways
this world holds
all our hearts

This Day a Gift

I accept this
day as a gift
no more something
to get through
overcome
push aside

I sit with you
and with myself
feeling into
how it is now
three years after
you left your body
to be burned

rubbing the sore places
clinging to sadness
wanting the ache
and wanting it to
anyhow somehow
disappear

can I let the gap be
slowly heal
open to
new space
for what
may come

and now
seeing this
asking this
I open the window
to sunshine
and the first
hints of spring

Possibility

I myself
am so
slow-growing
I want
evidence of
the always
possibility
of blooming
so I take photos
of flowers
in hope
of
myself

High Wind in Early Spring

Birds fly backwards
flipping out and over
sign posts fling down
roll in riot across
footpaths
eddies whirl up
from dry-as-dust fields

tall tree tops
shake quake
sway
trunks bend
fling small branches
about and dance
leaves in
mad wild rush

feeling eased by
wildness and riot
my heart opens out
to let go
of inner turmoil
turns
facing into the wind
to dance
the dance of the wilding
of the earth

Carrying Each Other's Loads

The memorial site
memories of you
projections of
love gratitude
the harness of the road
you carried a load
of dreams ambitions,
hopes and fears
heavy near the end

that day you wept
over words of praise
felt inadequate—
even — unbelievably —
ashamed — wept
hard tears
for the heaviness
of this unsought load
of others' dreams and desires
when there were more than
enough of your own

maybe I carried your
shadow together
with my own
the projections
of our sons' dreams
desires rage
the other face of
the love that is
in their bones

In Sight

Derailed
by wonder
tossed off the
line
of rational sense
splintered
into the
chaos of
flung forms
landing
at random
in wild beauty
the touching
of formerly
distant things
all knowing
feeling
being
akin

On a Bus

On a crowded bus
my hands rest
on the back of the seat
in front
almost touching
a man
broad shoulders
tall strong head
in an instant
my body floods with
longing for
those shoulders
that head
those fingers
the whole body
embrace
the hugging
my chin in the
remembered hollow
of your shoulder

The Morning of a Funeral

Familiar
the space
walking out the door
in black
ceremonial dress
rosary in hand
this too was
the space I held
for you

today's death is calmer
later older and kinder
but still that moment
of your departure
clings through
all the later
less-felt departures
of loved and known

The Work

The uncertain work
of excavation
my daily digging

to find
what I am
and where
tempted always
to stop

knowing
and loving
lie deep down
scattered   apart

the task
to find the courage
to hold space
for myself

to find
the honey
at my centre

where
confusion
of lived wisdom
waits in the dark

steeped
in silence
saved for this

to be freed into light
living food for the
knowing soul and
hungry heart

The Making of an Altar

No thundering
no flash of revelation
but the underground
burrowing deep
into the dark
slow growing
into conscious knowing
this is what I will do

gather all things
held sacred
now scattered in all
my rooms
bring them here
together
with his photo
an altar

so I began —
drawing together
all the scattered
sacred objects
the in-gathering to one
point — all the loved and
sacred held together
flanked by candlesticks

there I pray
and together with
this newly opened
prayer
the slow growing
in dark spaces
open into a
new knowing

we were together
side by side
sometimes one
growing into
and through
the blessings and pains
of our life
to meet
this first death

Prayer

May I
be with spirit
as with child
quickened in soul
lighteninged in heart
to dance the mystery
in every cell of
this body
all the days
of this
my every
life

Acknowledgement

These poems would never have found their way out of my computer, nor would this book have been conceived or created, without the invaluable help, support, and encouragement of my dear friend Pam Noda.

About the Author

Helen Fujimoto retired in 2011 after fifteen years as Associate Professor at the Japan College of Social Work, where she taught English (in English) and created General Studies courses (in Japanese) on such subjects as Intercultural Communication, War and Memory, International Social Work, and Migration from and to Japan.

Helen first came to live in Japan with her husband Akimi Fujimoto in 1980, after their meeting in Universiti Malaya. *Jalan Jalan: Life in a Malay Village,* is the story of their life in two Malay villages, written in English, translated into Japanese, and published in 1990. In 1998, the University of Foreign Studies published her Malaysian research, *The South Indian Muslim Community and the Evolution of the Jawi Peranakan in Penang up to 1948.*

Although Helen has written poetry for most of her life, *Singing the Seasons* is her first published volume of poetry.